CW00404302

FRANCIS FRITH'S

WALES

LIVING MEMORIES

Peter Thompson was born in South Africa, but has lived in Britain for many years. He read History at Aberystwyth and British Vernacular Architecture at Birmingham. He spends his time researching, recording and photographing historic buildings, and is dedicated to their appreciation and conservation. He also teaches local history. Peter Thompson lives in Barmouth in Gwynedd with his wife Paula and three children, where they also run a small hotel in their 17th-century farmhouse.

FRANCIS FRITH'S

PHOTOGRAPHIC MEMORIES

WALES
LIVING MEMORIES

PETER THOMPSON

First published in the United Kingdom in 2005 by The Francis Frith Collection

Hardback edition published in 2005 ISBN 1-85937-464-6

British Library Cataloguing in Publication Data

Wales Living Memories
Peter Thompson
ISBN 1-85937-464-6

The Francis Frith Collection
Frith's Barn, Teffont,
Salisbury, Wiltshire SP3 5QP
Tel: +44 (0) 1722 716 376
Email: info@francisfrith.co.uk
www.francisfrith.co.uk

Printed and bound in Great Britain

Front Cover: *Caernarvon, Castle Square c1955* C33082t
Frontispiece: *Pontardawe c1965* P183025

The colour-tinting is for illustrative purposes only, and is not intended to be historically accurate

As with any historical database the frith archive is constantly being corrected and improved and the publishers would welcome information on omissions or inaccuracies

CONTENTS

FRANCIS FRITH

VICTORIAN PIONEER

FRANCIS FRITH, founder of the world-famous photographic archive, was a complex and multi-talented man. A devout Quaker and a highly successful Victorian businessman, he was philosophical by nature and pioneering in outlook.

By 1855 he had already established a wholesale grocery business in Liverpool, and sold it for the astonishing sum of £200,000, which is the equivalent today of over £15,000,000. Now a very rich man, he was able to indulge his passion for travel. As a child he had pored over travel books written by early explorers, and his fancy and imagination had been stirred by family holidays to the sublime mountain regions of Wales and Scotland. 'What lands of spirit-stirring and enriching scenes and places!' he had written. He was to return to these scenes of grandeur in later years to 'recapture the thousands of vivid and tender memories', but with a different purpose. Now in his thirties, and captivated by the new science of photography, Frith set out on a series of pioneering journeys up the Nile and to the Near East that occupied him from 1856 unti 1860.

INTRIGUE AND EXPLORATION

These far-flung journeys were packed with intrigue and adventure. In his life story, written when he was sixty-three, Frith tells of being held captive by bandits, and of fighting 'an awful midnight battle to the very point of surrender with a deadly pack of hungry, wild dogs'. Wearing flowing Arab costume, Frith arrived at Akaba by camel sixty years before Lawrence of Arabia, where he encountered 'desert princes and rival sheikhs, blazing with jewel-hilted swords'.

He was the first photographer to venture beyond the sixth cataract of the Nile. Africa was still the mysterious 'Dark Continent', and Stanley and Livingstone's historic meeting was a decade into the future. The conditions for picture taking confound belief. He laboured for hours in his wicker dark-room in the sweltering heat of the desert, while the volatile chemicals fizzed dangerously in their trays. Back in London he exhibited his photographs and was 'rapturously cheered' by members of the Royal Society. His reputation as a photographer was made overnight.

VENTURE OF A LIFE-TIME

Characteristically, Frith quickly spotted the opportunity to create a new business as a specialist publisher of photographs. He lived in an era of immense and sometimes violent change. For the poor in the early part of Victoria's reign work was exhausting and the hours long, and people had precious little free time to enjoy themselves. Most people had no transport other than a cart or gig at their disposal, and rarely

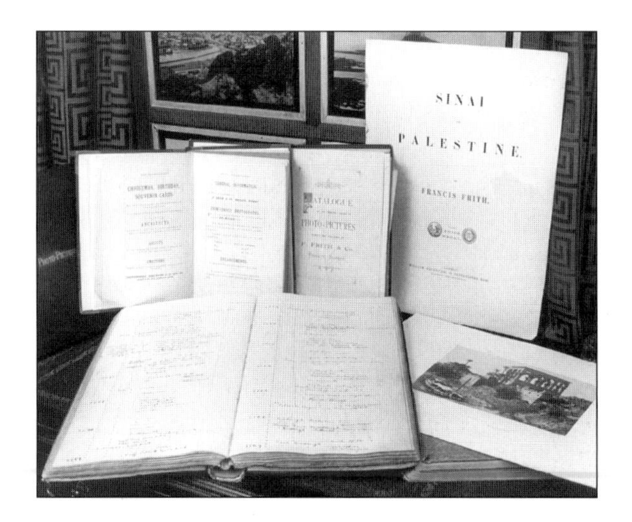

travelled far beyond the boundaries of their own town or village. However, by the 1870s the railways had threaded their way across the country, and Bank Holidays and half-day Saturdays had been made obligatory by Act of Parliament. All of a sudden the working man and his family were able to enjoy days out and see a little more of the world.

With typical business acumen, Francis Frith foresaw that these new tourists would enjoy having souvenirs to commemorate their days out. In 1860 he married Mary Ann Rosling and set out on a new career: his aim was to photograph every city, town and village in Britain. For the next thirty years he travelled the country by train and by pony and trap, producing fine photographs of seaside resorts and beauty spots that were keenly bought by millions of Victorians. These prints were painstakingly pasted into family albums and pored over during the dark nights of winter, rekindling precious memories of summer excursions.

THE RISE OF FRITH & CO

Frith's studio was soon supplying retail shops all over the country. To meet the demand he gathered about him a small team of photographers, and published the work of independent artist-photographers of the calibre of Roger Fenton and Francis Bedford. In order to gain some understanding of the scale of Frith's business one only has to look at the catalogue issued by Frith & Co in 1886: it runs to some 670 pages, listing not only many thousands of views of the British Isles but also many photographs of most European countries, and China, Japan, the USA and Canada - note the sample page shown on page 9 from the hand-written Frith & Co ledgers recording the pictures. By 1890 Frith had created the greatest specialist photographic publishing company in the world, with over 2,000 sales outlets - more than the combined number that Boots and WH Smith have today! The picture on the next page shows the Frith & Co display board at Ingleton in the Yorkshire Dales (left of window). Beautifully constructed with a mahogany frame and gilt inserts, it could display up to a dozen local scenes.

POSTCARD BONANZA

The ever-popular holiday postcard we know today took many years to develop. In 1870 the Post Office issued the first plain cards, with a pre-printed stamp on one face. In 1894 they allowed other publishers' cards to be sent through the mail with an attached adhesive halfpenny stamp. Demand grew rapidly, and in 1895 a new size of postcard was permitted called the court card, but there was little room for illustration. In 1899, a year after Frith's death, a new card measuring 5.5 x 3.5 inches became the standard format, but it was not until 1902 that the divided back came into being, so that the address and message could be on one face and a full-size illustration on the other. Frith & Co were in the vanguard of postcard development: Frith's sons Eustace and Cyril continued their father's monumental task, expanding the number of views offered to the public and recording more and more places in Britain, as the coasts and countryside were opened up to mass travel.

Francis Frith had died in 1898 at his villa in Cannes, his great project still growing. The archive he created continued in business for another seventy years. By 1970 it contained over a third of a million pictures showing 7,000 British towns and villages.

6	" St Catherine's College	+
7	" Senate House & Library	+
8	"	+
9	" Gerrard Hostel Bridge	+ + + +
30	" Geological Museum	+
1	" Addenbrooke's Hospital	+
2	" St Mary's Church	+
3	" Fitzwilliam Museum, Pitt Press &c	+
4	"	+
5	Buxton, The Crescent	+
6	" The Colonnade	+
7	" Public Gardens	+
8	"	+
9	Haddon Hall, View from the Terrace	+
40	Miller's Dale	+
1	Bakewell, Bridge &c	+
2	" Footbridge	+
3	" Church	+
4	" " Interior	+
5	Matlock Bath, The High Tor	+
6	" On the Derwent	+
7	" " Brunswood Terrace	+
8	" Cliffs at	+
9	" Cromford, &c from Black Rocks	+
0	Dovedale, Pickering Tors	+

FRANCIS FRITH'S LEGACY

Frith's legacy to us today is of immense significance and value, for the magnificent archive of evocative photographs he created provides a unique record of change in the cities, towns and villages throughout Britain over a century and more. Frith and his fellow studio photographers revisited locations many times down the years to update their views, compiling for us an enthralling and colourful pageant of British life and character.

We are fortunate that Frith was dedicated to recording the minutiae of everyday life, for it is this sheer wealth of visual data, the painstaking chronicle of changes in dress, transport, street layouts, buildings, housing, engineering and landscape that captivates us so much today. His remarkable images offer us a powerful link with the past and with the lives of our ancestors.

THE VALUE OF THE ARCHIVE TODAY

Computers have now made it possible for Frith's many thousands of images to be accessed almost instantly. Frith's images are increasingly used as visual resources, by social historians, by researchers into genealogy and ancestry, by architects and town planners, and by teachers involved in local history projects.

In addition, the archive offers every one of us an opportunity to examine the places where we and our families have lived and worked down the years. Highly successful in Frith's own era, the archive is now, a century and more on, entering a new phase of popularity. Historians consider the Francis Frith Collection to be of prime national importance. It is the only archive of its kind remaining in private ownership. Francis Frith's archive is now housed in an historic timber barn in the beautiful village of Teffont in Wiltshire. Its founder would not recognize the archive office as it is today. In place of the many thousands of dusty boxes containing glass plate negatives and an all-pervading odour of photographic chemicals, there are now ranks of computer screens. He would be amazed to watch his images travelling round the world at unimaginable speeds through internet lines.

The archive's future is both bright and exciting. Francis Frith, with his unshakeable belief in making photographs available to the greatest number of people, would undoubtedly approve of what is being done today with his lifetime's work. His photographs depicting our shared past are now bringing pleasure and enlightenment to millions around the world a century and more after his death.

WALES

AN INTRODUCTION

THIS IS a pictorial look at Wales, seen through the eyes of photographers, and comprises necessarily subjective impressions of places and people over a particular period. How did the land and history make Wales and the Welsh?

The adherence to a strong Celtic past is a principal theme of Welsh consciousness and forms part of their identity, is evident in much of their material heritage and persists tangibly in their language. When the Romans encountered the Druids on Anglesey they were not to be the last invaders experiencing difficulty in overcoming this fierce independence of will, language and terrain.

Only when Edward I built his ring of castles, from Harlech to Rhuddlan, in the north of Wales, and 'shire' his territories there, did a sense of order prevail. At least, that was, until Owain Glyndwr rose against the English in 1400 and inflamed the Welsh nation again until he, too was defeated nine years later.

If Welsh struggle was ended in 1409, Henry VIII's Act of Union of 1536 brought Wales into line with English law and administration and the official use of the English language. On paper at least, the Welsh became 'shareholders' to use a modern term. From this point we see Wales develop as part of England, almost, and it very much played its own part. That English fight for the throne, the Wars of the Roses raged in Wales too – it gave us the stirring song 'Men of Harlech'. The Civil War came to Wales too, and the nation played a great part in the religious upheavals of the following centuries. Quakers, persecuted in Dolgellau, in Meirionnydd, sailed to America at the end of the 17th century to found colonies and join William Penn in Pennsylvania. Wales was a foundation of the religious revival, of Methodism, during the 18th and 19th centuries and subsequently provided a great deal of radicalism to British politics.

If the early Welsh history is perhaps less well known, the idea of Wales as an industrial powerhouse is far more familiar. It can be said that the Industrial Revolution got under way in South Wales with the production of coal and iron and produced some of the first of the great magnates of the industrial age. The Guest family established ironworks at Dowlais in 1749 while the Crawshays did the same at Cyfarthfa, Merthyr Tydfil and building a huge iron empire.

The Bute family of Cardiff built their wealth on coal, iron and its transportation. Innovations in transport and communications, particularly with the construction of canals and the docks in Cardiff only made making their fortunes easier.

The importance of these magnates to the development of modern Wales cannot be overstated. The Rhondda Valley came to be the quintessential valley of the south Wales coalfield. In 1841, it had a population of less than 1000 and the only industrial activity within it was a little mining of house coal in its lower reaches. In the late 1840s, the Bute estate acquired the farm of Cwmsaerbren in the upper Rhondda. The valleys of Rhondda Fawr and Rhondda Fach came to have 40 collieries. The population peaked in 1924 when the Rhondda Urban District had 167,000 inhabitants, more than the combined populations of the counties of Cardigan, Meirionnydd and Montgomery.

In the north, too, heavy trades developed. Slate was quarried in Meirionnydd and Caernarfonshire on a vast scale and shipped all over Britain to put roofs on the houses of workers in many industrial areas. There were other industries also. Lead, tin and copper were extracted, as they had been for hundreds of years in some cases, from sites all over Wales and white gold was taken from mines near Dolgellau in Merionnydd. The 20th century continued this prodigious output, adding steel production at places like Llanwern and Port Talbot in the south and Shotton in the north. The images seen in this book tell of a Wales when this industrial activity was at one of its peaks. What sort of nation did this history produce?

The demography of Wales, especially in the south, was altered dramatically as workers sought work, and demand for labour in the industrialised communities meant that Wales experienced internal migration rather than mass emigration.

MONMOUTH, *Wye Bridge c1955* M91060

Between 1760 and 1914, some two-thirds of the population moved to live and work in the industrial south-east. Hard work in dangerous occupations led to a proud tradition of working-class radicalism – the Red Flag was first raised during the Merthyr Riots in 1831, whilst the Penrhyn lockout of 1900-03 at the Bethesda Quarries of Lord Penrhyn was one of the longest disputes in UK industrial history.

The harsh conditions, nevertheless, engendered a bond of common spirit that has become a watchword for these communities, one that is perhaps unique. Along with the radicalism there was a great desire for self-improvement, for learning too. The Cabans, or quarry mess rooms, became debating societies for the self-taught working man, libraries were funded by the men themselves and working mens' institutes were formed. Male voice choirs, perhaps the most distinctive theme tune the Welsh have had in the last half century, emerged from this culture.

This independent spirit fed into mainstream politics and first the Liberal and then the Labour Party benefited from this radical Welsh input. Indeed, Welshmen were responsible for some of the most significant social reforms of the 20th century; Lloyd George introduced the old-age pension in 1909, and Aneurin Bevan gave Britain the National Health Service in 1948.

It would certainly be wrong to believe that modern Wales is only about coal and industry. Most of Wales has continued with more traditional ways of life, and agriculture was still the main occupation. Farming is largely pastoral in most of Wales, with some dairy and only a little arable. Farms have tended to be run by owners, and some of them may have been worked by the same families for centuries.

The so-called Principality of Wales, although most would prefer to use the term nation, stretches from the Dee in the north to the Severn in the south, and encompasses a wonderful variety of rich, regional, often mountainous, landscapes, sometimes with cultures to match. From the Gogs* in the North, the Hwntw's** in the south and the Cardi's*** in the south west, the Welsh know how to rub each other up in a teasing sort of way.

There are distinctive parts to Wales. The borderlands that skirt Offa's Dyke and mingle a little with English counties have a gentler landscape with rolling lowlands, deciduous woods and a prosperous agriculture within easy communication with nearby major cities like Birmingham, Manchester and Bristol. There are industrial areas here, although fading now, such as the recently closed collieries at Bersham near Wrexham and reduced steel production at Shotton on Deeside, but it is a landscape of gentleness broken only by the hills rising towards Brecon in the south and the Clwyddian Range in the north.

The south east of Wales was the cradle to the Industrial Revolution, as we have seen, and was characterised by the production of coal, iron and steel, and the creation of whole towns was based on just one industry. These industries also demanded improved transportation, and a system of canals was threaded through eastern Wales and connected with England. Many of the photographs taken by Frith and his staff observe these closely-knit communities of the South Wales

* *Gogs* – from gogledd , north

** *Hwntw* – southern

*** *Cardi* – from Cardiganshire – by reputation a little parsimonious

valleys. When the photographs were taken no-one could ever have imagined that some of these monuments of industry would become a World Heritage Site and tourist attraction, such as 'The Big Pit' at Blaenafon (unfortunately not shown in this book), following the closure of much of the coal industry.

From its heyday in the late 19th century the coal industry suffered competition, both from cheap imports and alternative fuels like oil and gas, but the industry remained buoyant. By 1945 there were 33,000 miners in south Wales but by the 1990s there were less than a thousand, the final death knell stemming from the miner's strike of 1984-85. After that there seemed a determination to find alternatives to coal. Communities have been hard hit, and while European funding has been used to assist them long term solutions have not been easy.

The development of tourism has been one of the success stories of post-war Wales, although it has a long pedigree. There have always been notable travellers, like Defoe in the 17th century, and the 18th century saw a steady trickle of the well-to-do, but it was only with the laying out of railways from the 1860s and, later, the development of the motor car, that enabled greater numbers to come to Wales. Tourism has grown to be a major factor in the Welsh economy: it is now second only to agriculture in modern Wales. It is not difficult to understand the reason.

As we travel a little way from these industrial areas we enter a completely rural landscape of magnificent mountains and lakes, beautiful coastlines, wonderful estuaries and a vast array of hamlets, villages and small towns that have served their communities for centuries and give Wales and its people their identity.

The south and west of Wales, of Pembrokeshire, Ceredigion and Glamorgan is characterised by the many feudal castles– and a cathedral at St Davids - that remain. Castles such as Caerffili, Kidweli,

SAUNDERSFOOT, *The Harbour c1965* S64118

Carreg Cennen and Laugharne are smaller perhaps than those in the North but equally impressive. A rich agricultural landscape helps us to appreciate why the Normans were attracted here more than the inclement north. Fishing harbours such as Tenby, Solva and Fishguard, that look so tranquil now, have inspired for centuries with their absolute charm. The slightly larger market towns, like Carmarthen, Haverfordwest and Aberystwyth invite exploration without overwhelming the visitor.

The central areas of Wales offer remoteness and solitude in huge amounts and the towns that are there, such as Llandrindod Wells, Llanidloes, and Newtown all exist because of agriculture or small industries such as mineral production or woollen products, and have grown or survived because of the attraction they provided visitors from the 19th century onwards. This applies to much of rural Wales and particularly the north west. These have always been the least accessible areas, the last to hold out against invaders, the most difficult to work economically and the great bastion of the Welsh language. The attraction of the picturesque landscape to the English well-to-do from the 18th century onwards has persisted, and the English still come to stay and live here. Despite this, the great survival of the independently minded Welsh communities that continue to personify the region form a sometimes strange and grudging symbiosis with the incomers.

Heavily populated with tourists in the summer months, locations like Snowdonia, the Lleyn Peninsula and Anglesey and the coastal resorts like Rhyl, Llandudno and Barmouth, and the roads connecting them, groan with the burden of num bers, ever increasing since the War. Yet always in the hinterlands, remote, mountainous tranquillity remains to be enjoyed by those that seek out its pleasurable solitude.

As we hurtle into the 21st century, it seems that much of the economy of Wales is dedicating itself more to the pursuit of leisure and the needs of tourism, as farmers are encouraged to become stewards of the landscape while many of the traditional buildings in villages and farmland are converted into holiday accommodation or second homes. The dismantling of heavy industries also brings physical change to what we now see. Regeneration schemes are the rage now, like those in the Valleys and elsewhere, and bring light industry and landscaping of the spoil heaps. And who could blame those wanting to rid themselves of reminders of awful events like the Aberfan Disaster of 1964 when a coal spoil tip buried a school full of young children and killed a total of 144 people. Now the coal industry is dead and Wales adapts to different economic realities.

A book such as this clearly suggests there have been changes in industrial areas, but in many rural areas there have hardly been any changes at all. Nevertheless, there can be no doubt that we see a Wales that is slowly disappearing. The loss of jobs on the land and in industry has led to an exodus of people from Wales, while there has been an influx of outsiders bringing change to ways of life that are centuries old. Welsh distinctiveness is giving way to the 'corporate' uniformity that is promoted everywhere and has led to government schemes to restore a 'sense of place'!

The photographs that follow depict, with a few exceptions, the Wales of the decades following the Second World War. Like elsewhere in Britain, Wales was about to experience great changes in its economic and social life as it emerged from the privations of a war economy.

The end of the war brought a landslide victory for Labour, one that had great support from Wales. This was followed by years of Conservative rule and a buoyant economy. 'We never had it so good' was Macmillan's phrase. This period brought the creation of the Welfare State, new housing and education initiatives. The increasing demand for coal and steel meant the Welsh economy was buoyant – for a while. But aspects of daily life remained rooted to older ways, and the rural north and west, especially, was still mired in the social customs of a bygone age. As Dafydd Wigley, former president of Plaid Cymru remembered 'In many ways the 1950s was the end of an old era in Wales. It was still the shadow of the chapel, the dominance of the chapel and that culture that went with it.' Yet it was the evocation of this culture in Saunders Lewis's Cymru Fydd (Wales Will Be) that led to the success of Plaid Cymru and the language campaign that saw the creation of the Welsh Language TV channel S4C in 1980. Against this the great changes in British popular culture was to challenge these old ways. Rock 'n' Roll, pop music, television, the social mobility afforded by the motor car and post-war ideas that things had to change all helped unpick the sometimes dead hand of tradition.

The photographs here merely observe those not so distant places in time and the people that lived there. Street scenes are remarkably un-modernised and the absence of heavy traffic, or in some cases any traffic at all, is a delight to look at. But the scenes are not that different from what we could observe today, and we can easily identify with them because in time they are still within living memory. As they say, the past is a foreign country, so enjoy your journey to a place not too far away.

BALA, *High Street c1965* B7200

FROM CHEPSTOW TO BRECON AND SWANSEA

CHEPSTOW
The Town Gate and the George Hotel 1957 C77127

The Town Gate, rebuilt many times over the life of the town, has had many uses; at one time tolls were collected here for all manner of goods and livestock. The wonderfully curved building on the left accommodates Brenda's, a ladies' wear shop. Two police constables direct traffic through the narrow gate which, it has been said, 'survived not only the storms of centuries, but the profanity of the drivers of heavy motor vehicles'.

CHEPSTOW
Beaufort Square 1957 C77135

'Chepe' and 'stowe' combine to mean 'market place', which indicates the early origins of this town. Beaufort Square tells us something of the aristocratic involvement and patronage of the Beaufort family. The Square has many buildings dating back to the 18th and early 19th centuries. Next to the Square's war memorial (out of view) stands a captured gun from a German First World War submarine, which was presented to Chepstow in recognition of the bravery of Able Seaman Williams VC, a Chepstow man killed during the landings at Gallipoli.

TINTERN, *The Abbey c1955* T53051

The Cistercian abbey, founded in 1131, was enlarged several times over the course of its life until it was dissolved in 1536. There can few ruins as picturesque, and its setting has inspired artists of all kinds since the Reverend William Gilpin praised it in his guidebook 'Observations on the River Wye' in 1782. This photograph, taken before the inundation of visitors that that sometimes steals some of its magic, in the summer at least, captures perfectly the scene that inspired the sentiments expressed by Gilpin and others.

MONMOUTH, *St Thomas's Church c1965* M91092

This view shows the Monnow Gate that stands on the bridge of the same name to the left. However, the subject of this photograph is the church, dedicated to Thomas a Beckett, the Archbishop of Canterbury murdered in 1170, although the first church here may have been Saxon. By 1965 the church had undergone a number of changes through its long life, after several re-modellings. In 1233 fire damaged the church and the gatehouse (seen to the left here) during the battle of Monmouth, and 13 oaks were supplied to repair the church. In 1830 the church was restored by Thomas Henry Watt, and re-fashioned in brick with a turret being added. In 1874 John Pritchard, a former assistant of Pugin, removed the turret and replaced the brick with stone again. The vestries were added in 1887/88. The present east window dates from 1957.

MONMOUTH
Wye Bridge c1955
M91060

The beautiful bridge at Monmouth is perhaps less famous than its sister Monnow Bridge, but it is still nevertheless performing admirable service here. It was rebuilt in 1617. Monmouth is in the heart of the border country. Henry V was a son of the town and is commemorated by Agincourt Square, perhaps the finest monument to the king. Another famous son was the Honourable Charles Stewart Rolls; he was the first man, in 1910, to pilot a double crossing of the English Channel, although his finest legacy was to co-found the Rolls Royce company.

HAY-ON-WYE, *The Bridge c1965* H392106

Y Gelli Bridge, built of concrete, is a very modern introduction into the Welsh landscape. Nearby Hay has become renowned over recent decades as a 'book town' where every other shop seems to sell second-hand books. This began in 1961 when Richard Booth opened his first second-hand bookshop. The town's annual Hay Festival is now internationally famous with the literati.

CHAIN BRIDGE

The Bridge c1955 C571004

The village of Chain Bridge is on the River Usk. The design and construction of this interesting steel bowstring arch bridge (by John Webster, built in 1906), was the subject of an article in 'The Engineer' in 1907. Here two drinkers enjoy an outdoor tipple, gazing at the water and the chain bridge in this idyll of a rural scene.

PONTYMISTER

The Canal and the Bridge c1950

P309004

This delightful bridge spans the Monmouthshire canal. The canal was built between 1797 and 1812 to link Brecon with Newport and the Severn Estaury. Stone and processed lime from nearby quarries was transported by tramway to the canal and then by barge to Newport. At Pontymister an iron works was founded in 1801 and tin plate works later in the 19th century. The canal had fallen into disuse by the 1930s but has been gradually restored by the British Waterways Board, with support from the National Park and others since 1968; it was reopened to the public in 1970.

THREE COCKS
Mill Stores Cafe c1965 T343027

Many businesses grew from the tourist trade that came to Wales in the post-war decades. The name of this café, and the two grinding stones from the mill that lean by the doorway, explain the changing nature of the countryside in these decades.

BRECON
High Street c1955 B192056

Brecon is a well-manicured town on the River Usk with a smart range of buildings, mainly of the Georgian and Victorian periods, as we can see here. The military presence in the town and the museum of the South Wales Borderers - even the 13th-century cathedral was semi-fortified, which is most unusual - has perhaps helped maintain a sense of order. The South Wales Borderers were famous for their part in the action at Rorke's Drift in the Zulu Wars. The Brecon Beacons have been used extensively to train troops in the arts of combat simulation and survival techniques.

NEATH

Orchard Street and the Gwyn Hall c1950 N5011

The Gwyn Hall, on the left, was built in 1887. The land was donated by Hywel Gwyn, and a statue of him was unveiled outside a year later. The building was used for Council business as well as a music hall until the construction of the Civic Centre in the 1960s. In 1967 the statue was moved to allow a road widening that did not materialise, and in this photograph it points to the building opposite, Gwyn's birthplace, which was demolished in the 1960s to make way for Woolworths.

CRICKHOWELL
Beaufort Street c1955
C188095

Crickhowell is most famous for its grand 17th-century bridge over the Usk, and the nearby 1481ft Table Mountain. On top of Table Mountain is a 2,500-year-old fort (a crug) of Hywel, from which the town derived its name. In later years Crickhowell has become a busy base from which to venture out onto the Brecon Beacons, either on foot or by car. On the right of the photograph is the imposing Clarence Hall. Built in 1892, it was named after the Duke of Clarence, who laid the foundation stone in 1890. It has functioned as a concert hall and meeting-house. The near absence of motor cars makes street scenes such as this seem quite alien to us now.

detail of C188095

NEATH
Looking towards Victoria Gardens c1960 N5022

In the foreground there appears to be an event at the YMCA, and the general view over the municipal park shows another gathering in the gardens, perhaps related to the same event. The gardens were created in 1897, one of several physical expressions of civic pride engendered by economic confidence and prosperity in the town, and due undoubtedly to the benefits of industrial and commercial expansion in the 19th century. Neath's population grew from 3,000 in 1823 to 14,000 in 1880.

▼ **NEATH**

New Street c1965 N5050

A Mini, a Wolseley, a Ford Capri and Cortina, a Morris Traveller and others all suggest the age of the motor car is finally with us; this street is dominated by the motor vehicle. Sander's tobacco shop is typical of its time, when this sort of business used to flourish but is very rare now. Wandering into one of these specialist establishments one was almost overwhelmed by the sweet aromas of the tobacco products on sale.

► **ABERTILLERY**

General View c1955 A279024

This town was almost completely formed and defined by the production of coal. Like many of the towns in Wales that grew because of the extractive industries such as coal and slate, Abertillery expanded at an astonishing rate from 6,000 in 1881 to over 40,000 in 1921. This massive increase came from those seeking work in the town's coal mines, both from other parts of Wales, industrial and rural, and from the west of England, particularly Somerset and the Forest of Dean. The new housing built for the workers can be seen rising up the hill like a tide.

CWM
The Town Centre c1955
C517003

The 1950s were always bright and sunny halcyon days, weren't they? A young man trundles a push chair up the hill on this warm-looking afternoon.

RUMNEY
Llanrumney Estate c1965
R297023

Many estates of what we now call social housing sprang up around Britain following the war. The long rows of new council houses can be seen on the right of this picture, while the older, more substantial houses appear on the left. Much of the local authority housing was pretty cheerless in design, but it satisfied a great demand in the decades following the Second World War, due both to war damage and slum clearance in nearby Cardiff.

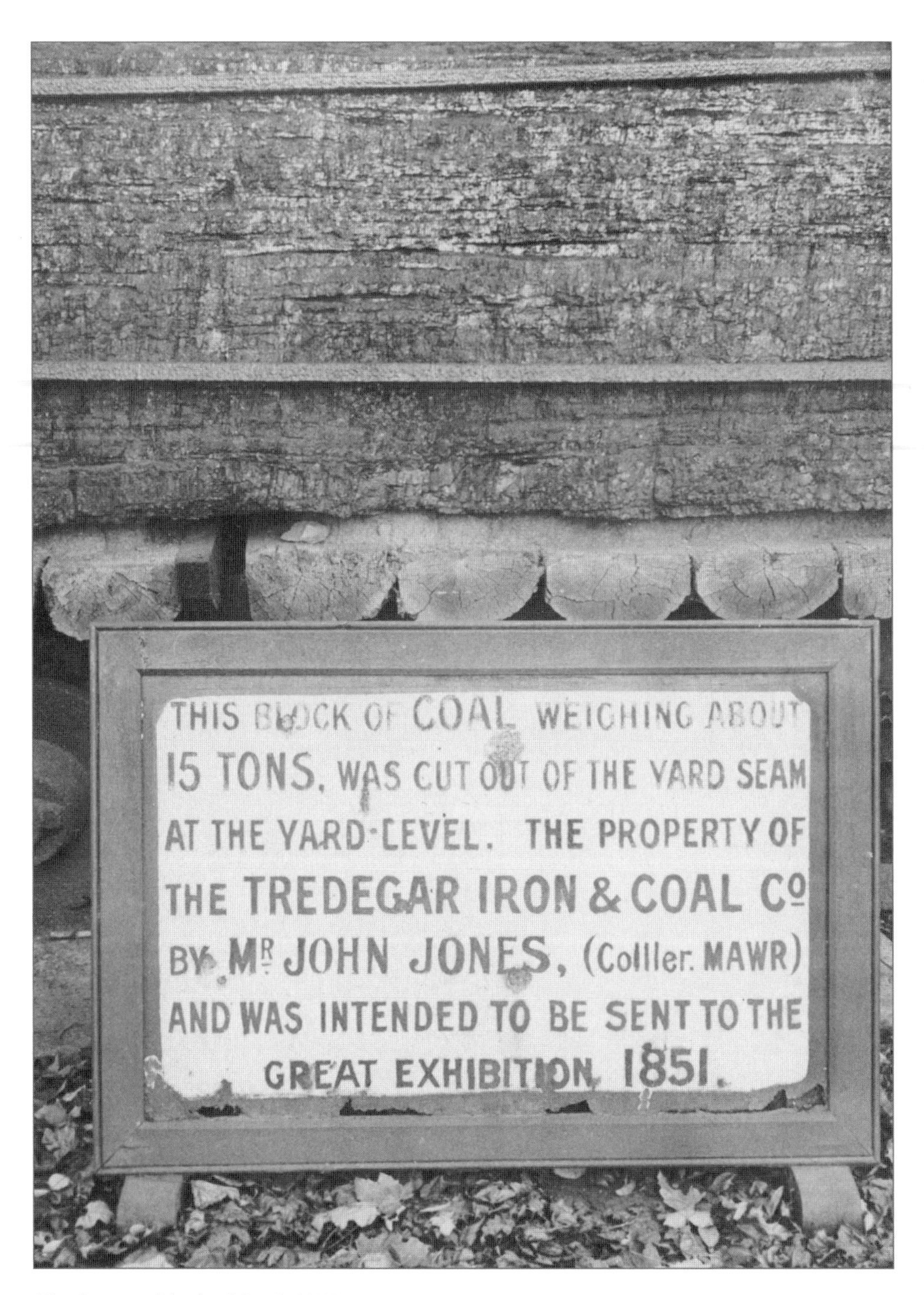

TREDEGAR, *The Largest Block of Coal c1955* T265013

Aneurin Bevin, Tredegar's most famous son, wrote of the coalminer's lot: 'In other trades, there are a thousand diversions to break the monotony of the work - the passing traffic, the morning newspaper, above all the sky, the sunshine and the rain. The miner has none of these. Every day for eight hours he dies, gives up a slice of his life and buries himself'.

TREHERBERT
Bute Street c1955
TI96007

This haunting, empty street is named after the coal magnate Lord Bute, a man of fabulous wealth, who shaped much of what industrial South Wales became during the 19th and 20th centuries. He built the first dock in Cardiff to ship out coal, and the first load ran by train from Treherbert in1855. This was the beginning of the Rhondda Valley as a major producer of coal.

TREORCHY, *The Square c1955* T197067

Timothy Whites, the chemist, was a familiar sight in post-war Wales and is a conspicuous business on the Square. Treorchy has suffered all the vicissitudes that every South Wales coal industry community has suffered in the 20th century, and now unemployment is a sad statistic. One product of the town has shone out like a beacon during this period, however. The Treorchy Male Voice Choir must be regarded as one of the success stories in the cultural history of Wales.

THE BABY SHOP
LEILA DANIEL
WATERS
BABY SHOP
KEEP
LEFT

MAESTEG
Talbot Street c1955
M210014

Maesteg is a town defined by its one time principal industry - coal. By the mid 1980s, most of the mines had shut, with dire consequences for the communities here. However, all that was still to come at the time when this photograph was taken. Here there is little to suggest the upheavals that would come as the people of the town go about their business. Growing trade in the town had led to the building of Talbot Street in the 1890s. The King Alfred pub, which is situated on the junction with Commercial Street, belies the fact that new leases for Talbot Street excluded public houses.

ST ATHAN, *The Village c1955* S435032

St Athan is home to RAF Athan, and has formed part of the local community and economy for many decades, particularly following the Second World War. It has grown steadily in recent times as other bases have been reduced or closed. The parish church, the cottages and the café selling petrol to the occasional motorist or serving refreshment to some tired cyclists reveal the slow pace that has now ceased to exist for most of us.

DINAS *The Square c1960* D31071

In the distance a Mini car is parked, which dates this photograph to 1959 or later. Evocative of days gone by, there is nice detail in this scene, such as the tractor with its passenger and the old vans. This village is situated near Barry, in the Vale of Glamorgan. The general newsagent and the petrol vendor make every effort to provide for the locals, even to the extent of the outdoor scales for the weight conscious.

CARDIFF
Duke Street and the Castle c1955 C23084

The castle has a long pedigree, with some remains of the Roman period imbedded within the structure, but the whole medieval core was systematically upgraded by the 3rd Marquis of Bute and his architect and designer William Burges in the 19th century. Structures such as the clock tower were added and interiors were transformed to reflect the Victorian taste for medieval and religious art and symbolism. Yet the family who had done so much to establish Cardiff,had driven the South Wales coal industry, had built the gothic fancy Castell Coch, and boasted an estate of 22,000 acres passed on a mere £437 as an inheritance in 1947, as family fortunes declined. By this time much of the Bute land had already been donated to the city.

CARDIFF
St Mary Street c1960 C23159

The city was and is the capital centre of Wales, and this importance has increased - it is now a modern commercial and administrative centre for the nation. This relatively peaceful and rather provincial scene has now given way to real city hustle and congested traffic. Royal Arcade on the right is the oldest arcade in the city, which links The Hayes and St Mary Street. Built in 1858, the arcade is a fantastic example of opulent Victorian architecture, with some original shop fronts still surviving.

CAERLEON
Goldcroft Common
1949 C4019

A solitary figure wanders towards the common in a Wales slowly recovering from the Second World War. The attractive mixture of village vernacular and Victorian buildings suggests a sleepy backwater, yet Caerleon has been an important site since Roman times, when they turned it into a major fortress, and the town now possesses the only remains of the legionary barracks in Europe, home of the Second Augustan Legion.

BARRY
Knap Boating Lake c1960
B27086

Knap is located in the quieter area of Barry, and here we see a very genteel-looking boating lake. Barry was to become one of the busiest of resorts on the south coast of post-war Wales.

CAERLEON
Gloucester Court 1968
C4040

The fact that this town has a Roman amphitheatre and a long history perhaps suggests why the new development seen here has been given the name Gloucester Court. Its name refers to the influence of the Earl of Gloucester, Lord of Caerleon. Typical of this type of development, a parade of useful shops is included for the convenience of the new residents. While these were a thoughtful, addition, they did not always compensate for the anonymity that such new housing schemes brought.

NEWPORT, *Ye Olde Murenger House c1950* N25139

What appears to be a medieval jettied building may be nothing of the sort. At one time said to be the site of the town house of the High Sheriff of Monmouthshire in the 16th century, the structure was almost certainly rebuilt during the 19th century. Some features of the original building have nevertheless survived in the rebuild, such as some ornate plasterwork. Whatever its pedigree, the building has served as a popular pub for many years and is an unusual and welcome alternative to the grander Victorian buildings on display around it.

NEWPORT
High Street c1950 N25140

Newport has a rich history, with Roman occupation at Caerleon, a medieval castle, and the Chartist Rising of 1839, which was put down by troops. However, it was as one of the powerhouses of Britain's industrialisation, producing vast quantities of coal, iron and, latterly, steel, that Newport became the town it now is. Hi-tech companies now fill the void left by the destruction of these heavy industries. Newport has become a busy sister city to Cardiff, with some good examples of Victorian architecture. Yet in 1951 there was a coal shortage that led to all shop windows being blacked out just a few years after the Second World War had demanded the same treatment! The few cars and heavy queues for buses seen here tell their own story about city transport and life in post-war Wales.

PORTHCAWL, *The Lower Promenade c1955* P79152

The promenade provides a curious facility that seems less user-friendly than we might expect today and is more akin to a stadium. Deck chairs on the paving and on the kerb above, concrete pillars, a wall to obscure the view and a rocky shore at high tide seem to invite only the intrepid holidaymaker. The town has its share of Victorian and Edwardian hotels, but the trend has followed the pattern of many such seaside towns, in having to decide what its market was and never quite succeeding in doing that.

SWANSEA
The Grand Hotel
c1965 S240224

The Grand has recently undergone a complete refurbishment and modernization, so this photograph reveals a little of its former tarnished glory following its heyday in the 1930s.

OXWICH
The Village c1965
O38094

Perhaps the girls are buying a bus ticket here, but the Walls ice cream signs suggest they may be after something more exciting. Walls and Lyons Maid were generally the only ice cream sellers on show in shops during these years. Nearby is the 13th-century Penrice Castle, which was originally built by the Normans after finally gaining control of the Gower in 1099.

detail of O38094

SWANSEA
St Mary's Church c1965
S240229

The St Mary's we see here was only a few years old, and is possibly the sixth church on the site. The 1898 version was completely destroyed in a wartime air raid, along with much of the town centre. This was in 1941 when most of Swansea – the 'ugly lovely' town of Dylan Thomas, was damaged beyond repair, including its historic 'Old Town'. The new building was re-opened by the Queen Mother on 28 May 1959.

SWANSEA *from the air 1959* AFA78437

LLANELLI, BUILTH WELLS, ABERYSTWYTH AND PEMBROKE

LLANELLI, *Stepney Street 1952* L73043

This view is remarkably similar today. The Burton's on the right is essentially the same shop front, although a different proprietor uses it now. Pedestrianisation and the dreary paving this inevitably brings, and a street-length covered walkway, would appear to be the main changes from the scene in the 1950s.

MORRISTON
The Cross 1954
M179036

This scene is little altered today. Billy Hole, whose newsagent's, stationer's and tobacconist's shop we see on the left, was an interesting character. As well as running this shop, he also operated a travel business catering 'for private party outings'. Billy Hole was a former Welsh soccer international who signed for Llanelli FC from Swansea Town during the latter stages of his career in 1929.

PONTARDAWE, *General View c1965* P183025

This photograph gives quite a rural impression of the town. From 1830, Pontardawe developed coal, iron and steel industries which drove the Industrial Revolution and helped make South Wales the economic power it was for much of the 20th century. The construction of the Swansea Canal, 1794-98, enabled the new industries to transport their goods, and although traffic on the canal all but ended in the 1930s, men were still working on the canal as late as 1950. The pop singer Mary Hopkin, a local Pontardawe girl, was to record 'Those were the days' a few years after this photograph was taken.

BUILTH WELLS
The Bridge c1955 B396054

This finely proportioned bridge was constructed in 1779 and widened in 1820. Builth grew up under the shadow of the castle, which was rebuilt by Edward I in 1277. Although a fire destroyed some 40 houses in 1690, the town as we know it flourished in later centuries owing to the attraction of its restorative spring waters, which led to 'Wells' being added to the town's name.

ELAN VALLEY
The Craig Goch Dam c1955
E185016

The fact that water is supplied from here still rankles with the Welsh – all this water is piped off to England. These dams were constructed from 1893 to 1904, and over 100 lives were lost during their construction; 50,000 people were involved in building them. More than 100 people in the valley also had to move to make way for the dams. Three manor houses, eighteen farms, a school and a church were demolished.

LLANIDLOES
A Flock of Sheep c1965 L403064

Near the middle of Wales, sheep are driven along a back road near the old market town. Llanidloes was one of the major centres for wool and flannel production from the late middle ages. That ubiquitous cottage industry of Wales has passed now, but farmers still tend their flocks. Nowadays they would be transported by lorry to their destinations.

STAYLITTLE
Clywedog Reservoir c1965 S621036

1965 saw the completion of this dam, which has made Llyn Clywedog Reservoir a nature lover's delight. The reservoir provides drinking water for consumers from Llanidloes to Bristol. At 72m, this it is the highest concrete dam in the UK, and was also intended to control the flow of water into the River Severn to help prevent flooding. The amount of water held back by the dam can apparently supply 555 million baths!

ABERYSTWYTH
The Beach c1960 A14382

A large pleasure boat beaches to unload its passengers, and a bandstand could still attract an audience in this university town cum resort in West Wales. In the background we can see the funicular railway for those not wanting to make the 485-foot walk up Constitution Hill. Former students of the college have a tradition of walking the promenade and 'kicking the bar' - the railings at the far end.

ABERYSTWYTH, *Terrace Road 1964* A14401

The photos displayed in the window of WH Smith (left) give us a flashback of the pop stars of the mid-sixties - Gene Pitney, the Bachelors, and possibly a newish group called the Beatles. Boots (in the middle distance on the right) is also still with us, but the Coliseum cinema beyond is now a good museum of the town's history. The Central Hotel, next to Freeman, Hardy & Willis on the corner, is popular with students, but the young man walking down the road would now be unwise to try this today!

ABERAERON
The Harbour Wall c1955 A182055

The harbour was built owing to the foresight of the Reverend Alban Gwynne following the enabling 1807 Harbour Act, and he spent his wife's inheritance building the planned Georgian town to go with it. Watching these young ladies walking along the harbour edge, it is difficult to imagine how busy a tourist spot this small town of brightly coloured houses was to become. The corn merchants and the Red Lion Hotel on the left still vie for trade from a rural economy that would change dramatically in favour of fancy ice cream and chic hotels.

ABERAERON, *Main Street c1955* A182062

This scene suggests that before the advent of modern tourism there was little to disturb the peace, and a dog could safely wander the streets without fear of traffic. Two people have time to chat, and perhaps the barber's shop on the left has some customers to attend to. For real excitement, the show jumping at the show advertised in the shop window on the right beckoned.

NATIONAL
CAFÉ
TEAS

LAMPETER
High Street c1955
L204029

Wales's oldest university is located here; it was established in 1822, and has brought a cosmopolitan complexion to this ancient and most distant of towns. Yet Lampeter has been able to retain its Welsh identity despite these influences. This post-war photograph belies the part the town played in the war, for in the district was a prisoner-of-war camp in Henllan, an RAF base at Llanon, the Land Army was based in Felinfach and parts of the town were commandeered for various uses. A pil box remains to this day as a reminder of the Nazi threat.

CENARTH
Coracle Fishing c1960 C376016

An audience watches from the old bridge as two coracle fishermen cast their nets for salmon or sea-trout. Sturgeon have also been caught here. Trying to land a 300lb, 8-foot fish from these small craft would seem a hazardous task, but it was once done in 1896 on the River Towy, overturning two coracles and breaking three nets in the process.

GWBERT-ON-SEA,
The Beach and the Cliffs c1955 G172007

'What a view!' is still the cry from the Cliff Hotel, and it is difficult to argue - these buildings perch on the cliff tops. The great attractions here, apart from the scenery, are the colonies of grey seals near Cardigan Island and the bottle-nosed dolphins.

▲ **NEVERN,** *The Village from the Bridge c1955* N116020B

The church of St Brynach, probably 6th-century and rebuilt by the Normans, and the early Celtic cross which stands 13ft high in the churchyard were the main attractions of this delightful village.

◄ **DINAS CROSS**
Cwm-yr-Eglwys c1960
D228050

This small hamlet enjoys a hundred or so metres of beach enclosed by a rocky cove in an idyllic setting. It has been very popular as a holiday retreat, and indeed nowadays most of these houses are holiday homes. All who have come gaze at the remaining gable of the small ruined church of St Brynach. It was completely destroyed by a terrific storm in 1859, which also destroyed some 144 ships.

FISHGUARD

The Lower Town c1955 F28043

This very attractive fishing port used to be a busy port for agricultural and fish product exports. The impressive harbour with its fine breakwater was constructed in 1906, in an effort to entice the great sea-going ships away from Liverpool and Southampton, but this idea came to nothing. Fishguard is famous for the defeat and capture of a French 'invasion force' in 1797, by the women of the town! The French force, which comprised a rag tail collection of drunken troops and released prisoners, attempted to land near the town. Hundreds of the town's women had donned scarlet clothes in order to look like soldiers, and this bluff, together with the effects of the alcohol, forced the French to surrender. One group of women, headed by a 'Jemima Fawr', and armed just with pitchforks, caught a dozen soldiers. This incident has the distinction of being the last invasion of British soil by a foreign power.

ST DAVID'S, *Cross Square c1955* S14050

The early cross which gives the square its name is prominent here, but the top of the tower of St David's Cathedral can be seen beyond the buildings on the right. Established in AD550, St David's is the birthplace of St David, and the cathedral was built in the valley where he worked. St David's is the smallest city in Britain and has drawn pilgrims for a millennium and a half.

▲ **SOLVA**

From the Gribbin c1955 S413015

This photograph was taken at a time when Solva's harbour was reaching the end of its time as a working harbour - the quay with its array of small boats looks somewhat run down. Solva was to become a haven for pleasure boats, and many of its houses were to become smartened up as holiday cottages. It is a welcome stopping place on that much travelled trail, the Pembrokeshire Coastal Path. The Gribbin is a steep, rocky headland overlooking the harbour and the spectacular Pembrokeshire coast.

◄ *detail from S413015*

PENDINE
The Beach c1955
P205081

You would not imagine from this picture that this area is dominated by caravans and seaside souvenir shops. In 1927 Malcolm Campbell achieved a land speed record of 174.88 mph on Pendine Sands. Unfortunately, a month later his Welsh rival, J G Parry-Williams, was killed attempting to beat the record.

LLANRHIAN
Abereiddy c1960
L267017

This is a quintessentially Welsh west coast environment, exposed, and enjoying little vegetation. Low, single-storey whitewashed cottages face up to the marine elements. They are now often turned into holiday homes, and are sometimes unfortunately modernised, with the loss of all the simple rough-edged character on display here.

MARLOES, *The Post Office c1955* M204007

Marloes village and the sands that are so attractive to holidaymakers were well served by this charming little building. It served as the post office and general stores until around 1965. The wonderful sandy beaches of the Sands have a backdrop of stunning rock formations in shale and sandstone. Holidaymakers may not always have known about the 130 or so Iron Age hut circles that exist on Gateholm Island, accessible at low tide.

CARMARTHEN
Fair Day c1950 C31037c

Carmarthen was granted its first charter in 1313, and it was the largest town in all Wales in the early 18th century. Now it is a busy market town, but without the pretensions of grandeur it might have had. This photograph was taken on fair day, when horses are being traded. In the 1950s horses still had some part to play in working the rural landscape, although their days were numbered.

CARMARTHEN, *The Old Oak 1949* C31052

The old stump of this tree known as Merlin's Oak is still kept in the town's civic hall. Even though the tree died in 1856 and the stump was finally dug up in 1978, people still attach a particular importance to it, as it was linked to the fortunes of the town. The old saying goes: 'When Merlin's Tree shall tumble down, Then shall fall (or drown!) Carmarthen Town'.

MAENCLOCHOG
The Village Shop c1955
M203009

This Pembrokeshire store sports a veritable Aladdin's cave of goods from whitewash to ice cream, and from newspapers to cake and cigarettes. Some buildings made of corrugated iron are now listed as being of architectural or historic interest. The railway station is Maenclochog was also constructed of corrugated iron and outlasted the railway itself, which closed down completely in 1949.

NARBERTH, *Commercial Corner c1955* N115002

Narberth has seen much change since this photograph was taken, and a great deal of redevelopment has taken place. Narberth was once part of the domain of the powerful medieval Mortimer family. On the right a Corona van is being loaded for its delivery runs, while a group stand around outside the Commercial Inn and something has distracted the children outside the grocer's.

AMROTH, *The Beach c1960* A187048

The AA sign on the Amroth Arms beckons as a recommendation in this pleasant Pembrokeshire village. Nearby Amroth Castle is a grand 18th-century house that sits on the site of Amroth's original Norman fortress, just yards from Amroth beach. Amroth had developed in the 19th century as a coal-mining village. A great storm in the 1930s washed away some of the cottages that stood on the seaward side of this road.

SAUNDERSFOOT
The Harbour c1965 S64118

From the entrance of the enclosed harbour, the village looks the perfect small beachside resort. Its quaint, colour-washed cottages complement the easy access to the beach. It is hard to imagine that the harbour was mainly used for the export of anthracite and coal. It was constructed after 1829, and it exported coal and iron from seven collieries in the vicinity which ceased production in the 1930s. Coal may have been extracted here since the 14th century.

TENBY
The Harbour c1925
T23008

Tenby is probably the most recognisable seaside town in Wales. The town walls date from the 13th century, and Tenby's tight, sheltered harbour and truly golden beach wears a crown of coloured Georgian buildings. The town developed as a Victorian watering hole for the well-to-do, especially after the railway came in 1863, but in post-war years it has been the destination for mass-tourism, mainly from the south midlands and the west county. The harbour is used to this day by a good mix of pleasure craft and working boats and, as this scene from 1925 shows, this has been the case for many years.

CALDEY ISLAND
The Priory Church c1965 C373040

Caldey Island, not far from Tenby, was settled by Celtic monks in the 6th century and was twice given to the Benedictine order, first in 1136 and once again in 1906; it has remained with the Benedictines ever since, who manage to make a living by selling produce and taking a limited number of visitors.

BOSHERSTON
The Tea Gardens c1955
B468060

Near Broadhaven and amidst unwelcoming military ranges, the village of Bosherston caters for visitors who enjoy walking and touring. The proud proprietors here, with their stylish new garden furniture, await their guests.

HAVERFORDWEST
Bridge Street c1955
H41013

An ancient town situated on the River Cleddau, it has succumbed to modernisation in recent years. Haverfordwest first developed when the Flemings established a town here and built the castle. Henry Tudor also passed this way with his army on the way to Bosworth to defeat Richard III. Here we see a very clean Bridge Street lined with interesting buildings – the street tempts us to explore its secrets.

HAVERFORDWEST, *Salutation Square c1960* H41080

The large war memorial dominates the square in front of the County Hotel. There are three such memorials in the town to remember the dead in foreign lands, but the town itself has seen action on its own soil. The castle resisted many attempts by the Welsh to take it, but a French force fired the town in 1405 when it landed to support Owain Glyndwr. The Marian martyr William Nichol was burnt at the stake in 1558, and Cromwell ordered the destruction of the castle during the Civil War.

MILFORD HAVEN
The Swimming Pool c1955 M77018

The modern Milford Haven grew in the 1790s and the port was to cater for the needs of the whaling ships, as they brought their cargoes here to be processed in blubber oil. Dockyards were also created here for the Navy. As these activities moved away, Milford reinvented itself from the 1880s as a true fishing port. This trade declined as well, despite the landing of a record catch of 60,000 tons of fish in 1946. Milford then turned to oil again, but this time a different kind of oil, and four oil refineries came into production from the 1950s, making Milford the second largest oil refining port in Europe in the 1970s. This was not without hazard, as the disaster of the spillage from the 'Sea Empress' at Milford in 1996 was to show. With the boats and quays in the background, this open-air swimming pool has a definite industrial maritime feel to it, but that did not prevent it from being very popular.

ANGLE, *The Village c1955* A188001

This enticing street is lined by woods on one side. There is a marvellous sense of past in this photograph with the rustic service station and long line of old cottages that flank the crenellated Globe Hotel.

PEMBROKE DOCK
The Car Ferry to Neyland c1960 P203057B

Brunel used Neyland as a terminus to connect to Ireland and the Atlantic, and his imprint remains everywhere, such as the name Brunel Avenue. He constructed a railway yard on a platform of floating pontoons. Neyland remained a railway terminus until 1955. A busy car ferry, the 'Cleddau Queen' seen here operated to Hobbs Point until the Cleddau bridge opened.

PEMBROKE, *Main Street c1955* P22005

The castle, re-built in stone from 1189 by William Marshall, Earl of Pembroke, keeps a broody watch on the town - as it has always done. Henry Tudor, the future King Henry VII, was born here in 1457. After years in exile under the protection of his uncle Jasper, Earl of Pembroke, Henry eventually brought the Wars of the Roses to an end when he defeated Richard II at Bosworth in 1485. It is fitting that Henry landed his invasion force of 55 ships and 2,000 mend amongst loyal supporters near Dale, not far from Pembroke.

PEMBROKE *from the air 1962* AFA104812

LLANDRINDOD WELLS, WREXHAM AND PRESTATYN

LLANDRINDOD WELLS
Temple Street c1950 L145086

The Metropole Hotel, beloved as a modern day conferencing venue and purveyor of Victoriana, looks a little sleepy in this post-war photograph. Llandrindod Wells developed in the 19th century as a spa town for the Victorian traveller, and hotels like the Metropole flourished. The influx of visitors was curtailed by the First World War. Tourism was also hampered by the depression of the 1920s, and there was to be growing competition from the other seaside resorts after the Second World War which would diminish visitor numbers further. At the time this picture was taken the town was in something of a decline, therefore, but was determined to recover – or regenerate, as we say now – and in 1990 a plaque was unveiled that proclaimed the 'Revictorianisation of Llandrindod Wells Station'! The town has followed suit.

LLANDRINDOD WELLS
Station Crescent 1962
L145128

The prominence of brick buildings here demonstrates a late flourish in the development of this town: the railway brought both bricks and visitors to the town. The varied roofscape reveals a forward-looking spirit as the 19th century gave way to the 20th.

KNIGHTON, *The View from Kinersley c1960* K61065

In 1230 Knighton was granted a charter to hold markets, and the tradition continues today. Wives were even sold, the last in 1854 – for one shilling. The town's name in Welsh is Tref y Clawdd, meaning 'the town on the dyke', and indeed it is located on Offa's Dyke, that great earthwork that separated the Welsh from the English tribes of King Offa. George Borrow, in his 'Wild Wales', noted that 'it was customary for the English to cut off the ears of every Welshman found on the east of the dyke and for the Welsh to hang every Englishman found to the west'. Things are a little better these days. Knighton is so close to the border that its railway station and hotel sit in England. The photograph shows how prosperous this small town has continued to be; though very rural, there is plenty of light industry here.

Player's Please
M.E.PRICE
SENIOR SERVICE
Satisfy
CAPSTAN
NELSON
WOODBINE

KNIGHTON

High Street c1955 K61106

This clock tower was erected in 1872, and dominates this small junction in the town. Knighton has managed to preserve its charming juxtaposition of period houses as we see here, and shows a very interesting townscape. A small girl prefers her umbrella to the shade under the shop blinds on this warm-looking day in post-war Wales. The years since this photograph was taken have done little to change any detail seen here.

KNIGHTON, *Kinsley Wood ER c1965* K61171

The Forestry Commission planted different species to commemorate the coronation of Elizabeth II in 1953. At Kinsley Wood the ER was planted on both sides of the hill.

NEWTOWN
Broad Street c1960
N171065

The market was established in 1279 with a charter granted by Edward I, but Newtown's growth is due mainly to the application of technology to the cottage-based woollen industry. Factories were built for carding and spinning machines, and the town became a major centre for handloom weaving. Robert Owen, the social reformer, was born here and died here in 1858. The Bear Hotel seen here was one of the principal hostelries and dated from the 18th century. Sadly it is no more, having made way for a new shopping precinct, although the upper floor façade has been retained.

WELSHPOOL
Broad Street c1955
W471009

In a rather smart streetscape of mostly rendered buildings, how evocative these splendid old vehicles look. W Watkins, the contractors advertised on the side of the truck on the right, continue today, and so does the newspaper office behind. Milk is awaiting delivery somewhere, judging by the crate on the bike.

WELSHPOOL
The Mermaid Inn c1955 W471011

Originally known just as Pool, 'Welsh'; was added to differentiate it from the English Poole in Dorset. Welshpool has had an anxious history, situated on the border with England, and has been destroyed on several occasions. As if to emphasise this, a small timber-framed inn stands neatly between later, or modified, buildings in this ancient market town three miles from the English border in Montgomeryshire. The building, formerly the Black Boy, dates from the 16th century but the front elevation is part of the restoration work of 1890 by Frank Shaylor.

LLANFAIR CAEREINION
The View from Neuadd Lane c1955 L394024

The church of St Mary dominates the surrounding area. The town originally developed because of the local weavers, and also as a market town. Owing to its disrepair, the earlier 13th-century church was completely rebuilt in 1868 to the plan of the earlier church of 1239. In justifying the demolition of the old church in 1866-67, a report commented that the repairs had been 'patched up at different times, without skill or architectural taste: ancient carved stones were thrown into the masonry in several places as common stone'. The church was rebuilt by Edward Haycock of Shrewsbury.

LLANERCH, *The Zoo c1955* L245011

A summer's day visit to the country and a ride on an ancient tortoise - simple pleasures! Many small, enterprising landowners attempted to lay out 'zoos' and farm parks in the decades following the Second World War, and most vanished. The chance to give children the opportunity to feed and stroke the animals was irrestistible, although climbing all over a giant tortoise, as these children are seen doing here, would perhaps be unacceptable today.

LLANYMYNECH, *Main Street c1960* L407008c

Two women discuss some hot local gossip, perhaps. The enamel signs would make a modern bric-a-brac dealer drool, and the lorry is loaded with hessian grain sacks open to the sun. Meanwhile, cattle further up the road amble in the road at their own leisurely pace. The English-Welsh border runs right through the village, indeed it runs right through the middle of the Lion Hotel. When the quite recent Welsh ban on Sabbath day drinking was enforced, half the pub could serve alcohol and other was 'dry' on a Sunday. It must have been entertaining to witness!

CEFN MAWR

Crane Street c1955 C365001

This small town, now part of Wrexham, was a mainly working-class community supplying workers for the various industries and mines in the area. Tramlines used to run through the streets as stone was moved to build the nearby aqueduct at Trevor, which was completed in 1805. The names Crane Street and Crane Corner came from the use of the crane to transfer trucks onto the tramway.

GLYN CEIRIOG

The Village c1965
G164068

Lloyd George once described the Ceiriog Valley as a 'little bit of heaven on earth', despite the small Wynne slate mine in the village. Glyn Ceiriog remained a relatively unspoilt place, even after the Prime Minister's recommendation.

CHIRK
The Viaduct and the Aqueduct c1955
C366112

Although somewhat overshadowed by Pontcysyllte Aqueduct, the beautifully proportioned Chirk Aqueduct ranks as a major work in its own right. Built between 1796 and 1801 at a cost of £20,898, the aqueduct carries the canal 70 feet above the River Ceiriog for a distance of 710 feet. Running alongside the aqueduct is Chirk Viaduct, which carries the Chester to Shrewsbury railway line. Erected between 1846 and 1848, and rebuilt in 1858, it was the work of the Scottish engineer Henry Robertson.

LLANRHAEADR
Market Square c1955
L246025

This scene is virtually unchanged today. The cyclist outside the café on the left may wonder what the photographer is doing, but there is probably little else to grab his attention on a normal day here. Llanrhaeadr-ym-Mochnant's main claim to fame was its waterfall; it was also the home vicarage of William Morgan, the 16th-century translator of the Bible into Welsh.

LLANGOLLEN, *The Canal c1935* L76031

The canal was started in 1793 and was completed in 1805. It was originally called the Ellesmere Canal, but is now known as the Llangollen Canal. Built by Thomas Telford, it was constructed to carry coal, slate and limestone for fertiliser. Two women walk with a child along the canal, while further ahead the horse can be seen towing the canal boat in this scene of perfect tranquillity.

CARROG
The River from the Bridge c1960 C364039

The bridge was built in 1661. Carrog, or Llansantffraid Glyndyfrdwy, is in the heart of the lands of Owain Glyndwr, the marcher lord. Following a land dispute with Reginald de Grey, Owain proclaimed himself Prince of Wales and rose against the English in 1400. Few visitors now could guess of Carrog's involvement in some of Wales's most violent years.

WREXHAM
High Street c1955
W153023

This marvellous scene shows a Wrexham that has since lost some of its unified Victorian and Edwardian streetscapes with its banks and traditional shop fronts. The Golden Lion pub on the right had its earliest licence in 1684, became subdivided into shops but reverted to an inn again by 1740. Originally timber-framed, it was rebuilt again in brick, as seen here.

WREXHAM
Regent Street c1965
W153081

Marks & Spencer's (left) has been a constant presence in Wrexham at a time when town centres generally have been under perpetual threat of change. This area has now been pedestrianised, but looks no busier than it does in this photograph, taken at a time when traffic could pass through.

GRESFORD

The Plough c1960 G59016

While not obvious from this photograph, Gresford is most famous for the tragic mining disaster of 1934 when 266 lives were lost following an explosion and fire at the Gresford Colliery. The disaster had tremendous significance. The inquiry into the disaster led to three disagreeing reports in 1937 on the causes of the disaster and the owner William Bonsall was convicted on eight counts of breaking mining safety laws, yet he was fined a mere £140 with £350 costs. This led to Sir Stafford Cripps demanding the nationalisation of the industry, which ultimately came in 1947. Gresford Colliery closed in 1973.

HANMER, *The Village c1955* H287004

Hanmer takes the name of one of the great aristocratic families of the Borderlands. A number of late medieval timber-framed thatched cottages remain, such as the one shown here; Magpie Cottage was, and is, a much photographed symbol of the village.

MOLD
High Street c1955
M201032

The charm of post-war rural Britain is captured perfectly here. The Morris on the left advertises driving lessons, while another Morris van in front of it advertises the virtues of a local pedigree herd of Jersey cattle. The almost organic nature of the buildings here has yet to succumb to modernisation, yet Mold has had its share of industrialisation. The town grew in the 18th and 19th centuries through the productin of lead, coal and iron. The Wrexham Lager advertised on the right was the first to be brewed in Britain.

RUTHIN, *Clwyd Street c1955* R292077

The mock-Tudor building seen here gives little indication of the real timber-framed buildings that remain in the town, although most would have been destroyed when Owain Glyndwr proclaimed himself Prince of Wales in 1400 and sacked the town 'leaving only three houses'. The cars appearing here in St Peter's Square, where a roundabout now guides traffic, were to be followed by many more as car ownership increased from the 1950s.

DYSERTH
The Falls from the Gardens c1955
D139045

These spectacular waterfalls near Rhyl are the main reason that people visit Dyserth, and postcards of the falls have been sent by impressed trippers to all parts of Britain and further. The waters once attracted pilgrims and later powered a flour mill on this site. Early visitors came on horseback but a motor train (1905) brought passengers from Prestatyn for 3d.This picture must be one of the best photographs, clearly showing the falls and the well-kept setting that is provided for visitors.

CILCAIN
The Village c1955
C367041

This small village, set amongst the Clwyddian Range of hills, once boasted seven pubs; the shop we see here is a grocer and butcher. All the cottages in this terrace used to be the same design as the centre example with its distinctive chequered brickwork and curious extended porch.

DENBIGH
High Street c1955
D22093

The contrasting styles of urban architecture seen in modern Denbigh speak of its history and its regenerative powers; here, medieval and Jacobean frontages are replaced with Georgian and Victorian modernisations. The building at the end of the High Street is the old Town Hall, which dates from 1572; it was remodelled in 1780 and is now used as a library and museum. The parking arrangements would appear interesting today.

BANGOR-IS-COED
The River and the Bridge c1955 B458012

Boys stand in their boats and paddle near the rapids, while others fish around on the bank without a concern in the world, as boys have probably done here for centuries. The bridge which spans the Dee dates from around 1660 and is attributed to Inigo Jones.

RHYL
The Pavilion c1955
R27232

The Pavilion, built in 1906 as the North Wales resorts sought to improve their entertainment facilities, has become a firm Rhyl favourite over the years. The paddling pool in front of it is a precursor of the modern day Sun Centre, perhaps. The coats and the empty pool reveal few takers for its delights – it must be a cold day. Prince's International Circus is billed to appear at the Pavilion.

LLANASA
The Village c1955
L239013

The village was once the seat of the diocesan church of St Asaph (Llanasaph), which dated back to the 13th century. Before us we can see the church of St Asaph and St Cyndeyrn, and the building on the right is the former Gyrn Arms Hotel. By 1953 the end had come for this pub, which had served villagers since around 1685. Frank Parry, the 77-year-old publican, had taken it over in 1907. The Herald of Wales report of the final night stated: 'Although he won't be pulling points any more, Frank Parry will still be busy, for he is the village gravedigger. He has been for scores of years and can't get rid of the job. None of the younger men will take it on'.

PRESTATYN
The Holiday Camp c1955
P110147

You could get a week's holiday 'all in' for £8 15s around the time of this photograph, and full entertainment was included right next to the beach by the owner, Billy Butlin. Mass tourism was in full swing in the 1950s and 60s, but by the 1980s tastes had begun to change, and the camp closed.

WREXHAM *from the air 1924* AF11193

ABERGELE, ABERDARON AND MACHYNLLETH

ABERGELE
The Beach c1965 A10053

This scene has altered little since the picture was captured. Cars can still spill onto the beach, and small cafés still provide small-scale refreshments to visitors, although a sea defence has been added since. The popularity of the north coast beaches and the advent of mass tourism led to the stretch of coastline between Rhyl and Colwyn Bay being almost totally occupied with caravan sites, amusement arcades, bingo halls and similar outlets of a new popular culture.

LLANDDULAS *The Dulas Arms Hotel c1955* L69165

It was good to get back to the small pleasures in life after the wartime years, and this small hotel seems a popular watering hole near the North Wales coast. The popular Reliant three-wheeler on the right enabled many less affluent types to take to the road at this time – and a few enthusiasts!

RHOS-ON-SEA, *Rhos Road c1955* R265100

Rhos-on-Sea was the poorer cousin to nearby Colwyn Bay, yet it still manages an identity of its own. This parade of shops selling its goods to potential holidaymakers runs down to the small promenade; the atmosphere here seems refreshingly restrained. Rhos is less commercialised than some of its neighbours, and remains a gentle mix of resort and rural seaside town.

LLANDUDNO
Pink Farm Cafe
c1960 L71613

If only we could eavesdrop on their conversations. This was a very popular café near Llandudno, photographed when marketing meant painting the service you offered in bold letters on your roof! Waitresses in traditional Welsh costume brought you your tea and lemonade to enjoy al fresco - weather permitting!

COLWYN BAY
The Pier Pavilion c1930 CI41014

The summer exodus of holidaymakers to the seaside resorts of Britain made piers a popular and lucrative venture. The Victoria Pier has had a chequered history. Opened in 1900, it has been almost destroyed by fire in 1923 and 1933, but it was rebuilt on both occasions. The Pavilion could seat 2,500 for its popular entertainment. The 1950s saw its swansong and it closed in 1958, reopening briefly as a discotheque, but finally closing its doors in 1991.

CONWY
The Bridges c1960 C156325

This interesting study of old and new highlights the abstract lines of the various bridges - road, rail and foot - that span out from under the walls of Conwy Castle and illustrates perfectly the importance of this river crossing to the history and economy of North Wales. On the right is Robert Stephenson's tubular wrought iron railway bridge, which was opened in 1849. In the centre, Thomas Telford's beautiful suspension bridge of 1826 can be seen, and the road bridge on the left was built in 1958. What cannot be seen is the A55 which now uses a tunnel that travels under the River Conwy.

▲ **EGLWYSBACH,** *The Institute and the Bee Hotel c1955* E99003

Enamel signs for Brooke Bond Tea on the village shop, a hostelry called the Bee and a small cottage displaying signs for the Aberconwy Institute 1915 and Llyfrgell y Sir or County Library suggest localised services that have largely disappeared from many small villages today.

LLANDUDNO
The Great Orme Railway c1960 L71693

A hidden cable system, the same as is used by the San Francisco tramcars, hauls holidaymakers and enthusiasts up to the Great Orme, the headland that overlooks the Victorian town. The train was installed to exploit the tourist potential of the attractive yet relatively inaccessible Great Orme, and was opened in 1902. Is it the photographer or the journey that appears to be a concern to the occupants of the train? Llandudno is the archetypal genteel, middle-class British seaside town with its sweeping promenade, pier, grand hotels and public spaces. The whole town was conceived and planned by Lord Mostyn, the major estate holder in the region.

BETHESDA
High Street c1955
B77021

Bethesda, a village born of slate and the workings of the Penrhyn Quarry, has always had a vibrant community. This spirit is perhaps due to its history: the villagers were united by the infamous Penrhyn Lockout, when the quarry owner, Lord Penrhyn, locked his workers out, bringing them ultimately to heel by great hardship and starvation, an act that was never forgotten.

BANGOR
Garth Road c1965
B14122

Here we see new building in post-war Wales - new shops, a supermarket and offices in the form of a modern precinct. Beyond are new university buildings and the Theatre Gwynedd sprouting from the trees, showing a forward-looking spirit in this ancient cathedral city. Such modernisation has proved successful in helping attract students to its university campus in the decades following the war.

▲ **SNOWDON,** *The Summit c1955* S144101

The structure that sits on top of Snowdon has many critics. While it has intermittently afforded shelter and refreshment to those that make the summit, and with a train to the top these are usually legion, many feel that a rather crude box is hardly an edifice suited for what is essentially a national monument. The mountain is now owned by the National Trust, and there are new plans for a more organic-looking structure.

◄ **CAERNARVON**
Castle Square c1955 C33082

The great castle of Edward I overpowers this scene as, of course, it was originally intended to do, and its distinctive polygonal towers distinguish it from other castles that Edward built. Started in 1283 by Master James of St George, it was taken briefly when the Welsh revolted in 1294. It was later strengthened and work finished in 1330. The Welsh had to live outside the town walls. Here we see the modern town square filled with coaches for holidaymakers and locals alike. The fountain and the municipal flowerbed, splendid symbols of civic pride, are sadly no longer with us.

CLYNNOG, *General View c1955* C561054

The relatively large, early 16th-century Church of St Beuno dominates the small village of Clynnog in Caernarfonshire – this scene has altered little since this photograph was taken. The church, which has a wonderfully plain interior but a fine roof and misericords in the chancel, was a stopping place for pilgrims on their way to, or from, Ynys Enlli (Bardsey Island), the most important place of pilgrimage in Britain during the middle ages. It was said that two pilgrimages to Bardey were the equivalent of going to Rome.

ABERDARON
The Beach c1955 A269266

Almost at the end of the Lleyn Peninsula, this small village opens out onto the beach and Cardigan Bay. Here the few visitors that could make their way here enjoy a lazy day on the beach. Aberdaron's 12th-century church of St Hywyn was ministered for many years by one of the great Welsh poets of the 20th century (or any century), R S Thomas.

ABERSOCH
The Village c1955
A13078

This former fishing village, situated on the south coast of the Lleyn Peninsula, now hosts boats of a much more upmarket kind. In the 19th century there were active leadmines in the area at Llanengan which also used the harbour to ship out. At the time of this photograph, visitors had realised what a beautiful location this was and how good the sailing could be, but had made few intrusions en masse. This changed as the village became increasingly anglicised and is now very popular with visitors.

ABERECH
The Village c1955
A271025

A few miles from the old port of Pwllheli, this small village on the side of the river Erch would seem to offer little to the passer-through; but a few houses, a church and a small shop offering anything from Lyon's Fruit Pies to tobacco might be worth a visit to a post-war visitor to the Lleyn area. The two workmen at the end of the road might also like to pass the time of day with a friendly chat.

CRICCIETH
High Street c1930
C186086

A policeman is perhaps waiting to direct the vehicles and protect the pedestrians, unaware as they seem of the approaching car. The Victorians firmly established Criccieth as a rather genteel watering hole for the holidaying classes, and its architecture certainly reflects this to this day. Only the castle is a reminder of past conflicts between Welsh and English. A Welsh castle, built in the early 13th century, it was later refashioned by Edward I after he defeated the Welsh in 1282.

MORFA BYCHAN
Black Rock Sands c1960 M96141

Many a local will remember learning to drive for the first time on this huge beach near Porthmadog, although summer access is now a little more restricted than we see here. In less hospitable times old ships have washed up on this and similar beaches on this coastline after coming to grief in storms in Cardigan Bay.

▲ **PORTHMADOG,** *The Harbour showing Cnicht and the Moelwyns c1955* P93106

At the height of the great slate trade of the 19th century, slate was shipped out from Porthmadog harbour, and the town grew steadily because of this. This post-war photograph shows a very different scene compared to the way it looks today. The right of the harbour now accommodates some rather incongruous housing, while the warehousing on the left has also given way to housing. What can be seen in the photograph is how little the narrow-gauge Ffestiniog Railway had been developed: no tracks are visible, and all appears to be wasteland. Now it is a popular railway for tourists.

◄ **BEDDGELERT**
The Village c1955 B49273

This extremely attractive village lies in the heart of mountainous Snowdonia on the Glaslyn river, and this fine bridge has been a magnet for visitors, who came in increasing numbers following the war. Although a great centre for walkers, it is as well known for the legend attached to the village. Prince Llywelyn killed his dog, Gelert, after he thought the dog had killed his son. The Prince found that the dog had in fact killed a wolf in protecting the child, but by then it was too late! Gelert's grave – 'bedd' - gives the village its name. Sad to say, the story seems to be a 19th-century invention to put the place on the map for Victorian visitors - and holidaymakers have absorbed this tale ever since.

FFESTINIOG
Pont yr Afon Gam c1960 F21060

This isolated petrol station and café three miles from Ffestiniog proclaims itself the highest petrol station in Wales. Its isolated position has lent itself to appearing in several films - once as a sheep station in the Australian outback! A local farmer, who appeared in the film, recalls how two Australian tourists almost careered off the road when a road sign erected as part of the set pointed to somewhere they knew back home in Oz. Needless to say, they did see the funny side to this.

HARLECH, *The Castle and Snowdon c1960* H21039

Harlech Castle, built 1283-1290 for Edward I by Master James of St George, the military achitect, as a statement of his military power. Owain Glyndwr took the castle for the Welsh in 1404 and held it until 1409, and it was under siege again during the Wars of the Roses in 1460. The bravery of the besieged Lancastrians was lauded in the song 'Men of Harlech'. The castle also saw action in the Civil War, surrendering to Cromwell's force in 1649. Many will find the view beyond the castle interesting as it shows the present secondary school under construction, while the residential developments beyond have yet to take place and all we see is a large camp of tents.

DYFFRYN
The Village c1960 D190113

On the right is the busy village store run by the Foxwell family, who only recently gave up the business. The village is a stopping-point on the way north or south along the coast, with just a prehistoric burial chamber and some beautiful hill walks to delay the traveller - unless you were making for the large caravan sites that emerged following the war. Parked on the road further up the street is a Mini estate, which was first sold in 1960.

BARMOUTH, *The Promenade and the Beach c1960* B22226

A hugely expansive beach here means that it never fills up with holidaymakers in this popular resort and former fishing and trading port. The mound in the middle of the estuary is called Ynys y Brawdd; the current that developed between it and the shore at full tides was extremely dangerous, and claimed many lives until a barrier was built across to the island.

▼ **FAIRBOURNE**
Beach Road c1955 F1063

The village was developed by Mr McDougall of the flour company at the end of the 19th century as part of his estate, and Fairbourne has become a popular destination for holidaymakers from the Midlands since, although a little soulless in the winter months. Note the Isetta 'bubble car' on the left. Later made by BMW, it sported a 247cc motorbike engine and it was said you could record its 0-40mph time with an egg timer – it took one minute flat!

► **ARTHOG**
The Village c1965 A61008

Modern dormer windows tell us that 'home improvements' are on their way for these small Welsh cottages, and this lady offers morning tea and coffee in hers to visitors on their way to the beaches nearby at Fairbourne and Barmouth. These smaller single-unit dwellings, provided for labourers and quarrymen, are now disappearing fast, either through demolition or through complete and unsympathetic alteration, and they are particularly unsuitable for enlargement.

BARMOUTH
The Mawddach Estuary c1960
B22231

The approach to Barmouth along the estuary is one of the most spectacular scenic routes in Britain, and it has inspired artists and visitors for centuries. Even a monument to the industrial age, the iron railway bridge, merely seems to enhance this journey. This donkey's eye view is not the best way to appreciate the bridge, perhaps, but the splendid backdrop of the Cader range of mountains beyond the river leaves little to be said.

GANLLWYD
The Tyn Y Groes Hotel c1955 G253036

This 19th-century inn has always catered for the anglers who frequent the fast-running waters of the Rover Mawddach in the Coed y Brenin forest near Dolgellay to catch their salmon and trout. Without the modern wide road that now snakes by, this scene looks charming and peaceful.

DOLGELLAU
The Regent Cafe and Filling Station 1956
D39313

A Little Chef and a more modern fuel station (the Mile End service station) has now taken the place of this homely café we see here offering teas and the delights of the ubiquitous Hovis loaf. This filling station was situated on a narrow road that twisted into the town of Dolgellau. The desire to improve communications has not been kind as the modernised A470 bypasses the old market town altogether.

BALA
High Street c1965
B7200

The medieval borough and market town of Bala is still loved for its wide streets in this most rural part of Meirionnydd. Bala has a Roman fort near the Lake and a Norman motte, but it was the production of hand-knitted woollens that put Bala on the map, even supplying George III with stockings for his rheumatism.

MEIFOD, *The Village c1960* M285050

This fine village could support its own bank (the white-painted building in the centre) in 1960. Today it is a private house. The Lloyd family, who set up Lloyds bank, came from Meifod – but the bank in the photograph is the Midland! The Lion Hotel, earlier called the Lion Inn, can be seen to the left.

DINAS MAWDDWY
The Village c1955 D30077

The recently afforested mountains near Dinas changed the landscape for a generation. Distinctive Welsh woollen cloth was manufactured at the mill in the village, and has latterly become a tourist outlet for these products. Dinas Mawddwy is also infamous for the murder of one Lewis Owen, Baron of the Exchequer and Vice Chamberlain of North Wales. He was put to death by a group known as the Red Bandits or Gwylliaid Cochian (on account of the colour of their hair) of Dinas Mawddwy in 1555. They were notorious for making raids and causing mayhem in a wide area, and Owen had attempted to curtail their activities.

CWM LLINAU

The River c1960 C558006

A ruined cottage is now only a place for lambs and the inquisitive to investigate.

TAL-Y-LLYN

General View c1965 T2086

This is one of the most photogenic and scenic of valleys in Wales, but it is never crowded. The range of houses and outbuildings offer some refreshments, and the odd fishing boat to hire. All the buildings have been converted in latter years to provide accommodation in an upmarket hotel complex. Nevertheless, the facilities on offer here remain unaltered - angling in complete peace and tranquillity, and refreshment. All this is now operated by the local water company, diversifying from their usual pursuits.

MACHYNLLETH
Maengwyn Street c1955 M3091

There are no trees obstructing the road now, but otherwise this scene has altered little and markets are still held. The newsagent on the corner survived until recently, and the post office has moved up the road a little. The workers on the right are putting the world to rights, and bread was brought to the door by the van of J G Jones. The town was shortlisted for the capital of Wales in the 1950s, which seems rich when it is compared with Cardiff, but may have something to do with its central location and the fast that Owain Glyndwr held a parliament here in the early 15th century during his valiant revolt against the English.

ABERDOVEY
The Beachfront c1935 A8099

Like many of the small resorts on the west coast of Wales, the largely Victorian seafront enjoys a very seasonal existence. Its original trade was as a fishing port, and 16th-century accounts tell of a great throng of boats assembling from 'around the kingdom' for the annual herring season. It must have been very different from this scene of holidaymakers on the beach. Modesty still demanded a few changing huts, and the overcoats some people are wearing suggest a determination to enjoy despite the weather!

TOWYN
Tal-y-Llyn Railway c1960 T67188

The resurrection of the narrow gauge railways in Wales has been one of the success stories of the tourist industry, and has rewarded the determination of the army of enthusiasts that operate them. The Tal-y-Llyn railway was used originally between 1866 and 1946 to haul slate from the Bryn Eglwys quarry at Nant Gwernol down to Tywyn Wharf station. Only four years after its closure enthusiasts had it running again, this time carrying passengers only.

ANGLESEY

BEAUMARIS, *The Cottage Cafe c1955* B44132

This extravagant jettied veranda is an amusing addition to this catering establishment, which attempts to afford some additional dining space at the expense of the traditional facades we see in the rest of the scene. The town is best-known for its castle of Edward I, started in 1294 in response to Madog's revolt, but never completed. Beaumaris has become a retreat for genteel visitors, and its fine mix of period buildings has contributed to this, but this appearance belies the importance of the maritime trade that took place here.

PENTRAETH
The Village c1965
P317042

This scene is virtually indistinguishable today: even the tear-shaped flower bed has survived decades of traffic management. The Panton Arms (left) is named after a local antiquarian, Paul Panton. Panton had married a local heiress, Jane Jones of Plas Gwyn, and they owned much of the estate around Pentraeth. Charles Dickens stayed here when reporting on the shipwreck of the 'Royal Charter' in 1859. By 1965, Pentraeth was a village that began to owe much to tourism, as the beach ware on sale at the shop on the right shows.

AMLWCH, *Dinorben Square c1935* A274027

The creeper-clad Dinorben Arms Hotel (left) and the Eleth Hotel provided good quality accommodation in the 1930s. The Dinorban was first listed as a hotel in 1828 when it was called the Ty Mawr; it was used as a court house before that. In 1784 it was recorded that a young man, William Roberts, was stripped to the waist, placed on horseback and flogged all the way to the port and back for stealing. The town and port had prospered owing to the mining activity on nearby Parys Mountain, which was the world's largest copper mine during the 18th and 19th centuries. The Eleth Hotel was demolished in 1962.

BUS
STOP
NO
HRK 811

CEMAES BAY
High Street c1955 C317135

Once a main port on this part of the coast with important connections to Liverpool, this small picturesque harbour town is an attraction for sailors of a more leisurely kind these days. In this picture we see a charming street with a definite vernacular feel to it. Notice the small row of cottages on the right with its rendered roof and catslide dormers; the traditional shop fronts; the plain render; and the sash windows. This was long before the days when pebbledash and UPVc windows started to suck the character from such local scenes as this.

LLANDDONA
The Village c1955
L437015

The timeless occupation of harvesting oats, at one with nature when performed by man and beast, is seen here on Anglesey. Soon however the more versatile tractor was to make horses largely redundant in the countryside.

PENYSARN
The Ancient Copper Mines c1950 P275010

Copper was extracted by the Romans here, but the present mines in Parys Mountain, near Amlwch, date from the 18th century, and were claimed to be the largest in the world during the Industrial Revolution. The mines were about to close when in 1768 fresh deposits of the copper were discovered. The workings around this redundant engine room and chimney building are a fine – or grim- reminder of those glorious days.

HOLYHEAD, *Market Street c1955* H105216

Holyhead has seen a decline in recent years, although Swift was able to write in 1727 that it was 'scurvy, ill-provided and comfortless', so recent trends may have followed a pattern. Modern regeneration initiatives have not yet helped the situation, as the town utilised off-the-peg townscaping schemes even though these may attempt to ape earlier architectural themes. The town is an important ferry terminal *en route* to Dublin in Ireland. Here we see a very traditional streetscape, with original shop fronts and a unified feel uncluttered by the traffic of today.

INDEX

The Francis Frith Collection Titles

www.francisfrith.co.uk

The Francis Frith Collection publishes over 100 new titles each year. A selection of those currently available is listed below. For latest catalogue please contact The Francis Frith Collection. Town Books 96 pages, approximately 75 photos. County and Themed Books 128 pages, approximately 135 photos (unless specified). All titles hardback with laminated case and jacket, except those indicated pb (paperback)

Accrington Old and New
Alderley Edge and Wilmslow
Amersham, Chesham and Rickmansworth
Andover
Around Abergavenny
Around Alton
Aylesbury
Barnstaple
Bedford
Bedfordshire
Berkshire Living Memories
Berkshire PA
Blackpool Pocket Album
Bognor Regis
Bournemouth
Bradford
Bridgend
Bridport
Brighton and Hove
Bristol
Buckinghamshire
Calne Living Memories
Camberley PA
Canterbury Cathedral
Cardiff Old and New
Chatham and the Medway Towns
Chelmsford
Chepstow Then and Now
Cheshire
Cheshire Living Memories
Chester
Chesterfield
Chigwell
Christchurch
Churches of East Cornwall
Clevedon
Clitheroe
Corby Living Memories
Cornish Coast
Cornwall Living Memories
Cotswold Living Memories
Cotswold Pocket Album
Coulsdon, Chipstead and Woodmanstern
County Durham
Cromer, Sheringham and Holt
Dartmoor Pocket Album
Derby
Derbyshire
Derbyshire Living Memories
Devon
Devon Churches
Dorchester
Dorset Coast PA
Dorset Living Memories
Dorset Villages
Down the Dart
Down the Severn
Down the Thames
Dunmow, Thaxted and Finchingfield
Durham
East Anglia PA
East Devon
East Grinstead
Edinburgh
Ely and The Fens
Essex PA
Essex Second Selection
Essex: The London Boroughs
Exeter
Exmoor
Falmouth
Farnborough, Fleet and Aldershot
Folkestone
Frome
Furness and Cartmel Peninsulas
Glamorgan
Glasgow
Glastonbury
Gloucester
Gloucestershire
Greater Manchester
Guildford
Hailsham
Hampshire
Harrogate
Hastings and Bexhill
Haywards Heath Living Memories
Heads of the Valleys
Heart of Lancashire PA
Helston
Herefordshire
Horsham
Humberside PA
Huntingdon, St Neots and St Ives
Hythe, Romney Marsh and Ashford
Ilfracombe
Ipswich PA
Isle of Wight
Isle of Wight Living Memories
King's Lynn

Available from your local bookshop or from the publisher

The Francis Frith Collection Titles (continued)

Kingston upon Thames
Lake District PA
Lancashire Living Memories
Lancashire Villages
Lancaster, Morecombe and Heysham Pocket Album
Leeds PA
Leicester
Leicestershire
Lincolnshire Living Memoires
Lincolnshire Pocket Album
Liverpool and Merseyside
London PA
Ludlow
Maidenhead
Maidstone
Malmesbury
Manchester PA
Marlborough
Matlock
Merseyside Living Memories
Nantwich and Crewe
New Forest
Newbury Living Memories
Newquay to St Ives
North Devon Living Memories
North London
North Wales
North Yorkshire
Northamptonshire
Northumberland
Northwich
Nottingham
Nottinghamshire PA
Oakham
Odiham Then and Now
Oxford Pocket Album
Oxfordshire
Padstow
Pembrokeshire
Penzance
Petersfield Then and Now
Plymouth
Poole and Sandbanks
Preston PA
Ramsgate Old and New
Reading Pocket Album
Redditch Living Memories
Redhill to Reigate
Rhondda Valley Living Mems
Richmond
Ringwood
Rochdale
Romford PA
Salisbury PA
Scotland
Scottish Castles
Sevenoaks and Tonbridge
Sheffield and South Yorkshire PA
Shropshire
Somerset
South Devon Coast
South Devon Living Memories
South East London
Southampton PA
Southend PA
Southport
Southwold to Aldeburgh
Stourbridge Living Memories
Stratford upon Avon
Stroud
Suffolk
Suffolk PA
Surrey Living Memories
Sussex
Sutton
Swanage and Purbeck
Swansea Pocket Album
Swindon Living Memories
Taunton
Teignmouth
Tenby and Saundersfoot
Tiverton
Torbay
Truro
Uppingham
Villages of Kent
Villages of Surrey
Villages of Sussex PA
Wakefield and the Five Towns Living Memories
Warrington
Warwick
Warwickshire PA
Wellingborough Living Memories
Wells
Welsh Castles
West Midlands PA
West Wiltshire Towns
West Yorkshire
Weston-super-Mare
Weymouth
Widnes and Runcorn
Wiltshire Churches
Wiltshire Living memories
Wiltshire PA
Wimborne
Winchester PA
Windermere
Windsor
Wirral
Wokingham and Bracknell
Woodbridge
Worcester
Worcestershire
Worcestershire Living Memories
Wyre Forest
York PA
Yorkshire
Yorkshire Coastal Memories
Yorkshire Dales
Yorkshire Revisited

See Frith books on the internet at www.francisfrith.co.uk

Frith Products & Services

Francis Frith would doubtless be pleased to know that the pioneering publishing venture he started in 1860 still continues today. Over a hundred and forty years later, The Francis Frith Collection continues in the same innovative tradition and is now one of the foremost publishers of vintage photographs in the world. Some of the current activities include:

Interior Decoration

Today Frith's photographs can be seen framed and as giant wall murals in thousands of pubs, restaurants, hotels, banks, retail stores and other public buildings throughout the country. In every case they enhance the unique local atmosphere of the places they depict and provide reminders of gentler days in an increasingly busy and frenetic world.

Product Promotions

Frith products are used by many major companies to promote the sales of their own products or to reinforce their own history and heritage. Frith promotions have been used by Hovis bread, Courage beers, Scots Porage Oats, Colman's mustard, Cadbury's foods, Mellow Birds coffee, Dunhill pipe tobacco, Guinness, and Bulmer's Cider.

Genealogy and Family History

As the interest in family history and roots grows world-wide, more and more people are turning to Frith's photographs of Great Britain for images of the towns, villages and streets where their ancestors lived; and, of course, photographs of the churches and chapels where their ancestors were christened, married and buried are an essential part of every genealogy tree and family album.

Frith Products

All Frith photographs are available Framed or just as Mounted Prints and Posters (size 23 x 16 inches). These may be ordered from the address below. From time to time other products - Address Books, Maps, etc - are available.

The Internet

Already ninety thousand Frith photographs can be viewed and purchased on the internet through the Frith websites and a myriad of partner sites.

For more detailed information on Frith companies and products, look at these sites:

www.francisfrith.co.uk
www.francisfrith.com
(for North American visitors)

See the complete list of Frith Books at:
www.francisfrith.co.uk
This web site is regularly updated with the latest list of publications from The Francis Frith Collection. If you wish to buy books relating to another part of the country that your local bookshop does not stock, you may purchase on-line.

For further information, trade, or author enquiries please contact us at the address below:

The Francis Frith Collection, Frith's Barn, Teffont, Salisbury, Wiltshire, England SP3 5QP.
Tel: +44 (0)1722 716 376 Fax: +44 (0)1722 716 881 Email: sales@francisfrith.co.uk

See Frith books on the internet at www.francisfrith.co.uk

FREE PRINT OF YOUR CHOICE

Mounted Print
Overall size 14 x 11 inches (355 x 280mm)

Choose any Frith photograph in this book.
Simply complete the Voucher opposite and return it with your remittance for £2.25 (to cover postage and handling) and we will print the photograph of your choice in SEPIA (size 11 x 8 inches) and supply it in a cream mount with a burgundy rule line (overall size 14 x 11 inches).
Please note: photographs with a reference number starting with a "Z" are not Frith photographs and cannot be supplied under this offer.
Offer valid for delivery to one UK address only.

***PLUS:* Order additional Mounted Prints at HALF PRICE - £7.49 each** (normally £14.99)
If you would like to order more Frith prints from this book, possibly as gifts for friends and family, you can buy them at half price (with no additional postage and handling costs).

***PLUS:* Have your Mounted Prints framed**
For an extra £14.95 per print you can have your mounted print(s) framed in an elegant polished wood and gilt moulding, overall size 16 x 13 inches (no additional postage and handling required).

IMPORTANT!

These special prices are only available if you use this form to order. You must use the ORIGINAL VOUCHER on this page (no copies permitted). We can only despatch to one UK address. This offer cannot be combined with any other offer.

Send completed Voucher form to:
The Francis Frith Collection, Frith's Barn, Teffont, Salisbury, Wiltshire SP3 5QP

CHOOSE A PHOTOGRAPH FROM THIS BOOK

for FREE and Reduced Price Frith Prints

Please do not photocopy this voucher. Only the original is valid, so please fill it in, cut it out and return it to us with your order.

Picture ref no	Page no	Qty	Mounted @ £7.49	Framed + £14.95	Total Cost £
		1	Free of charge*	£	£
			£7.49	£	£
			£7.49	£	£
			£7.49	£	£
			£7.49	£	£
			£7.49	£	£
			* Post & handling		£2.25
			Total Order Cost		£

Please allow 28 days for delivery.
Offer available to one UK address only

Title of this book ....
I enclose a cheque/postal order for £ ....
made payable to 'The Francis Frith Collection'

OR please debit my Mastercard / Visa / Maestro / Amex card, details below

Card Number

Issue No (Maestro only) Valid from (Maestro)

Expires Signature

Name Mr/Mrs/Ms ....

Address ....

....

....

.... Postcode ....

Daytime Tel No ....

Email ....

ISBN: 1-85937-464-6 Valid to 31/12/08

Free Print - see overleaf

Would you like to find out more about Francis Frith?

We have recently recruited some entertaining speakers who are happy to visit local groups, clubs and societies to give an illustrated talk documenting Frith's travels and photographs. If you are a member of such a group and are interested in hosting a presentation, we would love to hear from you.

Our speakers bring with them a small selection of our local town and county books, together with sample prints. They are happy to take orders. A small proportion of the order value is donated to the group who have hosted the presentation. The talks are therefore an excellent way of fundraising for small groups and societies.

Can you help us with information about any of the Frith photographs in this book?

We are gradually compiling an historical record for each of the photographs in the Frith archive. It is always fascinating to find out the names of the people shown in the pictures, as well as insights into the shops, buildings and other features depicted.

If you recognize anyone in the photographs in this book, or if you have information not already included in the author's caption, do let us know. We would love to hear from you, and will try to publish it in future books or articles.

Our production team

Frith books are produced by a small dedicated team at offices in the converted Grade II listed 18th-century barn at Teffont near Salisbury, illustrated above. Most have worked with the Frith Collection for many years. All have in common one quality: they have a passion for the Frith Collection. The team is constantly expanding, but currently includes:

Paul Baron, Phillip Brennan, Jason Buck, John Buck, Ruth Butler, Heather Crisp, David Davies, Louis du Mont, Isobel Hall, Lucy Hart, Julian Hight, Peter Horne, James Kinnear, Karen Kinnear, Tina Leary, Stuart Login, David Marsh, Lesley-Ann Millard, Sue Molloy, Glenda Morgan, Wayne Morgan, Sarah Roberts, Kate Rotondetto, Dean Scource, Eliza Sackett, Terence Sackett, Sandra Sampson, Adrian Sanders, Sandra Sanger, Julia Skinner, David Turner, Miles Smith, Lewis Taylor, Shelley Tolcher, Lorraine Tuck, Amanita Wainwright and Ricky Williams.